15.95

D0929882

FLAGS OF
LOUISIANA

FLAGS
OF
LOUISIANA

By Jeanne Frois
Illustrated by Larry Pardue

PELICAN PUBLISHING COMPANY
GRETNA 1995

*The word "Pelican" and the depiction of a pelican are trademarks
of Pelican Publishing Company, Inc.,
and are registered in the U.S. Patent and Trademark Office.*

Library of Congress Cataloging-in-Publication Data
Frois, Jeanne.
    Flags of Louisiana / by Jeanne Frois ; illustrated
by Larry Pardue.
       p. cm.
    ISBN 1-56554-047-6 (hc)
    1. Flags—Louisiana—Juvenile literature.   I.
Pardue, Larry. II. Title.
CR114.L8F76   1995
929.9'2'0973—dc20   94-48699
                                       CIP
                                       AC

Manufactured in Hong Kong

Published by Pelican Publishing Company, Inc.
1101 Monroe Street, Gretna, Louisiana 70053

To the Boys of Normandy,
June 6, 1944,
living or dead

Contents

Acknowledgments

One of the most pleasant aspects of researching and writing this book has been the people with whom I've come in contact. Their interest, intelligence, and helpfulness were invaluable and enjoyable. To the following people, I extend my deep appreciation:

To Etta Frois, the original family researcher and my mother, for her incisiveness and unfailing support that went way beyond the "call of duty."

To Tim and Pat.

To Ms. Margie Miller of the Archdiocesan School Board, in memory.

To Ms. Claire O'Donnell.

To Ms. Sally Angers of the Mayor's Office, City of New Iberia (and the flagbearers).

To Ms. Karen M. Doran of the Mayor's Office, City of Shreveport.

To Mr. Todd Hymel of St. Louis Cathedral, New Orleans.

To Ms. Ann Kennedy of the New Orleans Public Library.

To Ms. Lauren LaBoeuf of the Children's Hospital Medical Library.

To Ms. Vannie Nettles of the Ouachita Parish Police Jury.

To Mayor Curtis Joubert, City of Eunice.

To Ms. Shirley F. Vigé, Senior City Clerk, City of Eunice.

To Ms. Ginny Moody, Assistant City Clerk, City of Eunice.

To the Police Department Detectives, City of Eunice.

To Ms. Judy Voelker of the Mayor's Office, City of Slidell.

To Ms. Pam Gaspard of the Mayor's Office, City of Abbeville.

To my editor, Nina Kooij.

To Mr. Robert Goodman of the Flag & Banner Company, New Orleans.

Special thanks to the Archangel, for all of the love, patience, and understanding—"My heroes have always been Cowboys. . . ."

FLAGS OF LOUISIANA

PART I

HISTORIC FLAGS
OF LOUISIANA

CHAPTER 1
The Spanish Flag

THE CASTLE AND THE LION
1492-1541

Louisiana, along with the other states of the Union, had its beginning when Christopher Columbus set sail for India, carrying with him the Spanish flag of Leon and Castile. He left Europe in 1492, in the midst of the Renaissance. Ruby-colored wine was being drunk from golden goblets at the court of Isabella and Ferdinand, and the nobility and people of consequence lived in castles and houses featuring arches, mullioned windows, and courtyards.

Columbus was ambitious with this hard-won mission. He did not intend to find a land where the persecuted of Europe could move to and be free. He wanted to become rich and famous by finding a western sailing route that led to the silks, spices, gold, ivory, and other treasures of India.

A thousand miles southeast of the point where the muddy waters of the Mississippi gushed into the blue of the Gulf of Mexico, Columbus reached the crystal waters and white beaches of the land he christened San Salvador ("Saint Savior"). The flag of Leon and Castile waved from his ships. It was a strong-willed, proud flag, as red and gold as an August sun.

It had reached far back in time for its colors. In the ninth century, the French king Charles I, the Bald (823-877), stood before the Count of Aragon after a battle and ran his blood-stained hand across a golden shield, streaking it with red. These became the colors of northeastern Spain, which was called Aragon.

On the Spanish flag Columbus carried, the golden castles of Castile, with their three towers, were flanked by the red lions of Leon, wearing golden crowns that resembled tongues of flames. Leon was an area in northwestern Spain whose name meant "lion." Castile, a region in central Spain, was filled with

The Spanish flag of Leon and Castile

many castles, which helped protect its people. Castile is a Spanish word meaning "castle."

The design of the flag had struck a fine balance between the rules of heraldry and the egos of the two proud provinces that had been joined together. The two most important places of honor on a flag are near the hoist and in the upper half of the field (see glossary). In order to avoid offending either province, the castle and the lion were both on the upper portion of the flag, with the gold castle on a red quarter being closest to the hoist. On the bottom half, the red lion of Leon on a white quarter was nearest the hoist. The castle and lion appeared twice on the flag and were placed diagonally so neither Leon nor Castile would be given more importance. And at the time of Columbus's voyage, Ferdinand and Isabella were the rulers of the two kingdoms.

In 1519, when Alonso Alvarez de Pineda sailed westward from Florida and reportedly reached the mouth of a great river that gushed from the northern shores of the Gulf of Mexico, the arms of Leon and Castile also flew from his ships' masts. In May 1541, Spanish explorer and conquistador Hernando de Soto carried the same flag with him as he searched for gold, nearly half a century after Columbus. Traveling overland in Columbus's New World, he reached a wide and muddy river at a point south of present-day Memphis, Tennessee, in what would later be claimed as the Louisiana territory.

He had reached an area peopled with the Natchez, Caddo, Acolopissa, Houma, Tensas, and Tunica Indian tribes. Alligators, other wildlife, and Indians killed most of de Soto's men. De Soto died not long after, wracked by malaria. His men were most afraid of the very hostile Indians around them, and they wanted to hide the fact that their leader had died. Weighting down his dead body, de Soto's men gave his remains to the greenish-brown depths of the Mississippi River. The great river that swallowed the one man who could have colonized its banks remained unknown to the Europeans for another century.

CHAPTER 2
The French Fleur-de-Lis

LILIES IN THE WIND
1672-1762

It almost seemed to be a sign of destiny. The iris, growing wild over Louisiana, regally lighting up the dark-green bayous, was the symbol of France. It began before Louisiana was discovered or even dreamed about, long before French Jesuit priest Jacques Marquette and the Canadian explorer Louis Joliet traveled the Mississippi. Years before these two explorers mistakenly believed they had found the great mythical river that supposedly spanned the New World from east to west, giving them a path straight to the treasures of China, the golden irises on the banner they carried had streamed in the winds of France. Since almost the beginning of her history in the year 496, France claimed the fleur-de-lis as the flower of her kings. This had begun with Clovis, the founder of the Frankish monarchy.

The Franks were Germanic tribes who lived east of the Rhine River in what is now Germany. From the time of the third century to the fifth century, these battling people invaded Gaul constantly. Gaul is an ancient name for the region of Western Europe now known as France, western Germany, and northern Italy.

Clovis, the leader of the Franks, was a pagan. He ruled people who worshipped ancient gods, or Roman gods, or no gods at all. He sought to bring the prosperous Gaul civilization under his own control. And when he went to battle, the sturdy, fierce, and no-nonsense King Clovis carried with him his standard: a plain white banner with three golden toads.

On the eve of what seemed to be a particularly hopeless battle for the Franks, Clovis had a dream. He was looking over his troops in their breastplates and helmets, with their shields, swords, spears, and axes. His own banner was streaming in the wind and as he looked up at its white field with the three golden toads, it changed before his very eyes. The three toads had become three beautiful golden lilies. The dream awoke him. It was the eve before the birthday of the God of his Christian wife, Chlotilde.

And then he was on the battlefield. In the middle of the clash of steel weapons and the death and wounding of men around him, Clovis vowed in his heart to Chlotilde that if he were the conqueror that day, he would acknowledge her God and become a Christian. Clovis and his troops routed their enemies, and the once nonbelieving Clovis was baptized into the Christian faith by St. Remigius in the cathedral at Rheims on Christmas Day. Clovis changed his banner from the three toads to the three lilies, which are actually believed to be the yellow iris, and carried these on the blue color of the Chape de St. Martin. *Chape* is a French word that means "cope." A cope is the long cape worn by priests during religious ceremonies.

During the next centuries, banners with the three golden irises, or lilies, on a plain azure field that was representative of the Chape de St. Martin were used from time to time by French kings. King Louis VII of France, a national hero because of his adventures in the Holy Land during the Crusades in the years

The Lily Flag of Bourbon France

1147-49, added the iris to his coat of arms. The common people worshipped him and shortened his name from Louis to Luce, then finally to "Lys." The long-stemmed iris was called "Fleur-de-Lys," or Louis's flower. However, fleur-de-lis, actually translated from French, means "lily flower" or "lily bloom."

For many years, the gold fleur-de-lis on an azure field remained the flag of France. However, when St. Louis IX (1214-70) of France was released from his capture in Egypt during the Sixth Crusade, he hoisted the golden fleur-de-lis on a brilliant field of white. But it was not until the 1600s, when France, under the Bourbon royal family, accepted Protestants, that the prevalent field of azure was changed to white, which was the color of the Protestants.

During the seventeenth century, King Louis XIV, also known as the "Sun King," declared without a shred of modesty that "the state is myself." The flag of Louis XIV was snow white, strewn with the three radiant fleur-de-lis. As he lived in the splendid gilt of the palace of Versailles, two ragged young explorers in the New World were winding their way down a mighty river the Indians called "Meche Sebe," through a countryside that could be called, at best, wild. Marquette and Joliet checked their compass every day hoping the river was carrying them west to the Pacific, but found it was forever going south . . . south . . . south. Thinking, in error, that they had reached the Great River's mouth where it met the Arkansas River, the explorers turned back. It was 1672.

Ten years later, René-Robert Cavelier, Sieur de La Salle, was canoeing down this same great river with eighteen Indians and twenty-three Frenchmen in tow. Passing the stopping point of Marquette and Joliet, La Salle and his group continued onward in spite of the extremely powerful current. Like stick boats bobbing on the water, the buckskin-colored and water-stained canoes were pulled down the forceful, deceptively peaceful looking Mississippi, all the way to the mouth of the river and its fertile delta, which La Salle quickly explored.

On April 9, 1682, La Salle, arrayed in his finest clothing, appeared before his men. In the stillness of a primordial new land, on a spring morning that gave no hint of the broiling summers to come, his men gathered around him—the Frenchmen dressed like musketeers and the Indians clothed in buckskin with feathers in the black iridescence of their hair. A cross was erected on Louisiana soil and, beside it, a pillar. Upon this pillar was placed the royal coat of arms bearing the fleur-de-lis as La Salle, "with the consent of the Indian nations," claimed for Louis, King of France, all of the Mississippi River, all of its tributaries flowing in or out, all lands watered and drained by these rivers—in short, all of middle North America that spread from the Appalachian Mountains to the Rockies. La Salle solemnly christened the vast stretch of earth he had just claimed for France "Louisiane," named for the Sun King who ruled from Versailles.

Shortly after, La Salle would be murdered by his own men.

For the next eighty years, the white flag with fleur-de-lis would fly over Louisiana. It flew high in the year 1698 as Pierre le Moyne, Sieur d'Iberville, discovered the mouth of the Mississippi River from a ship in the Gulf of Mexico on Fat Tuesday and named the site Point Mardi Gras. It waved in the wind when his brother, Jean Baptiste le Moyne, Sieur de Bienville, in 1718 began a French trading post on a crescent-shaped piece of land on the banks of the Mississippi. What later became the teeming metropolis of New Orleans was born. The deep curve of the river just past the site of New Orleans provided protection for the settlement because it slowed any approaching ships and exposed them to defending gunfire if necessary.

The Lily Flag of Bourbon France also saw the coming of the Jesuit priests, the Capuchins, the Ursuline nuns, and the "casket girls" who came from France to marry the lonely settlers and begin populating the colony. These girls had been given chests or "caskets" filled with personal belongings to bring with them to the New World.

If any of the French settlers held any feelings of condescension for the Indians of the area, it became apparent that they were also dependent upon them not only for labor, but for their very health. They were thousands of miles from civilization and

22

the accepted medical care of their time. The Indians, who had embraced nature as their life source, were very wise about the herbs and wild flowers that grew around them in abundance. At first they were reluctant to reveal their healing secrets to the French. But in time, the condescension and mistrust eased on both sides and the Indians began to teach the French about the magical powers of herbs.

The French gradually transformed Louisiana from a primeval jungle into a colony. From the 1720s to the mid-1730s, Indians and African slaves dug canals, constructed levees, and erected buildings. Since the lower Mississippi River valley had few stones, the rich clay and abundant timber of the region was used for brickmaking. The technique used for building was to set heavy wooden beams in an upright position and lay the bricks between the posts. Sometimes the settlers used the same "adobe" technique they learned from the Louisiana Indians: instead of bricks, a mixture of moss and mud, which later dried and hardened, filled the spaces between the wooden beams. Sometimes these moss houses were stained with colors. Wide plantation homes were built under graceful, sloping rooftops with shady and inviting porches called galleries. The galleries were usually as wide as the houses themselves. Louisiana houses very much resembled plantation homes of the West Indies.

France ruled the colony of Louisiana until 1762, when Louisiana was ceded to Spain in the Treaty of Paris, at the end of the French and Indian War. Until then, the banner that was born from a pagan king's dream more than twelve hundred years before gleamed in the tropical Louisiana sun, the yellow flowers on its white field matched by the wild purple Louisiana irises spilling over the land.

CHAPTER 3
The Return of the Spanish Flag

FIRE IN THE SKY
1763-1803

During the years after de Soto found the Mississippi, Marquette and Joliet had come along, and La Salle had claimed Louisiana (all the Mississippi River, its tributaries, and the land from the Rockies to the Appalachians) for France. The French had ruled it for eighty years. But by 1762, France was pretty sick of Louisiana. France had lost Canada to the British and this made Louisiana extremely vulnerable, expensive, and too difficult for the French to govern.

During this time, France's circumstances were closely tied with Spain's, since the kings were cousins. Spain had also lost an important territory to Great Britain: Florida. France saw a way to compensate the Spanish for this loss, while at the same time unburdening itself of its steamy stepchild, Louisiana. France ceded Louisiana to Spain on November 3, 1762. The results of the Treaty of Paris in 1763 gave all of the land east of the Mississippi River to England and everything west of the river went to Spain, except for New Orleans, which remained French.

But it wasn't until 1769 that the graceful flowered flag of France was replaced by the strong-willed colors of the flag of Spain. The symbols of Leon and Castile that had been so largely obvious in the Spanish flag of Isabella and Ferdinand were now reproduced in a small, crowned insignia near the hoist. The flag had kept the vivid red and gold of Aragon for its colors: two scarlet horizontal borders on the golden field. It was an elegant flag, simple in its design, yet still conveying power, like a fire in the sky. Despite the fact that most of Louisiana was now under Spanish rule, loyal French natives refused to take down the Lily Flag of Bourbon France.

When Canada was lost to England, the Acadians who lived on Nova Scotia were driven out by the British, undesirable

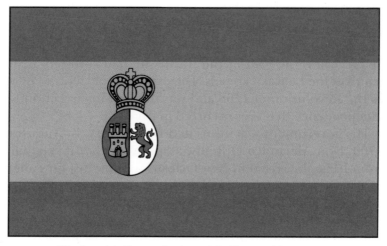

The Spanish flag at the time of the Treaty of Paris

mainly because of their Catholicism. The Acadians, or Cajuns, who arrived in Louisiana during the 1760s, joined their fellow Frenchmen in asking the king of France to cancel the cessation to Spain because they wanted to remain loyal to their mother country. While the French were clamoring to remain French, Don Antonio de Ulloa, a Spanish scientist with piercing black eyes, flowing black hair, and a slight build, arrived in Louisiana to become the first Spanish governor.

He announced he was taking possession of the province for the king of Spain, but he never presented his credentials to the ruling French authorities. This was a diplomatic mistake. In the eyes of the French and Acadians, this error reduced him to the status of crackpot.

What's more, after he had explored the Mississippi to where it met the Arkansas River, Ulloa decided to move to a tiny French military post named the Balize (beacon) at the mouth of the river, taking with him his new bride. He allowed the French flag to fly over Louisiana, hoisting the Spanish flag only at the Balize.

He was hated throughout Louisiana. The French and Acadians had formed what was called the Superior Council. In 1768, seeking independence, they demanded that Ulloa either present his credentials that showed him to be the true governor of Louisiana or get out. In November 1768, fearing for his safety, Ulloa fled the colony and returned to the court of Spain, where he told of the insults he had suffered at the hands of the Louisiana rebels. The expulsion of Ulloa is known as the Revolution of 1768 and was the first insurrection for independence that ever occurred in America.

His government was infuriated by the story. In August of 1769, Don Alejandro O'Reilly, a Spanish general originally from Ireland, arrived in New Orleans to show just how angry Spain was. Accompanied by a strong military, he took possession of all Louisiana in the name of Spain.

The French Fleur-de-Lis, which had flown in the Place d'Armes (Jackson Square) for the seven years since France had ceded Louisiana to Spain, was replaced with the blazon of Leon and Castile snapping briskly in the wind. Spanish flags were hoisted on every flagpole available. After honoring his Lord in the parish church of St. Louis, O'Reilly turned to the business at hand. He went after the leaders of the Superior Council.

Serving as judge at their trial, O'Reilly sentenced six men who have been called the "Martyrs of Louisiana" to death for sedition: Pierre Caresse, Nicolas Chauvin de la Frenière, Pierre Marquis, Joseph Milhet, Jean-Baptiste Noyan, and Joseph Villere. Five were put to death by firing squad on October 25, 1769, nearly a year to the date Ulloa had been expelled. Villere was killed either on a Spanish frigate or at the city gates. Six more were sent to prison in Havana but were liberated through the influence of the French government. Ironically, it was O'Reilly himself who pled for mercy for these men once he had left Louisiana for good.

In 1769, O'Reilly, proving that he would not be frightened off like Ulloa, replaced the Superior Council of Louisiana with a *cabildo* (council). *Louisiane* became the Spanish *Luisiana*, and its present-day name is a combination of the first two cultures that ruled it. The Spanish laws that so wisely governed the Indies and Spain's rich Caribbean empire were brought to wild Louisiana. Having pardoned the other revolutionaries, O'Reilly began forging diplomatic relations between the French and

Spanish. The former French—and quarrelsome—province became orderly and quiet, filled with justice.

Buildings of grace and beauty began replacing the shanty-like structures that had made some areas an eyesore. The Moorish influence on Spanish architecture—ornamental arches, balconies, and courtyards, some of which were filled with fruit trees—became apparent, especially in New Orleans. The delicate lacework of black wrought iron found in Spain and southern France began adorning the galleries and balconies in Louisiana, reproduced by slave labor. The French word *rue* became the Spanish *calle*, both meaning "street." In the streets of New Orleans, Indians sold herbal cures with other goods, and Africans grew these same herbs in their gardens.

The Place d'Armes, over which flew the flag of Spain, became the private property of Don Andrés Almonester y Rojas, under a questionable, very secretive chain of events that never came to light. He was a fabulously wealthy man, father of the much-desired Micaela, who became the Baroness de Pontalba. When St. Louis Cathedral was destroyed by the Great Fire of 1788, Almonester financed its reconstruction with his own money. Later, Gov. Baron Hector de Carondelet borrowed the money to build the Cabildo town hall from Almonester. The hurricane that destroyed sailor Jean Louis's 1736 Hospice des Pauvres, the forerunner of Charity Hospital, only spurred Almonester on to rebuild that as well.

Three times under Spanish rule, the city of New Orleans was consumed by an orange fury of fire. Its rooftops, made of thatch or shingles of cypress wood, were perfect fuel for the tiniest of sparks carried on the wind. After the fires of 1788, 1792, and 1794, Governor Carondelet ruled that only roofs made of tile could be built in the city.

From 1769 on, the colony began to prosper under the wise, exceptional, and dynamic Spanish governors who ruled through the end of the eighteenth century—Unzaga, Gálvez, Miró, Carondelet, Gayoso, Salcedo—until 1803, when once more Louisiana belonged to France, and the tricolor of the French Revolution flew briefly in the Place d'Armes.

CHAPTER 4
The British Flag

CROSSES
1763-1779

While the gilded castle of Castile and the blood-red lion of Leon were billowing over the western bank of the Mississippi in Spanish-held Louisiana, to the east of the Great River, in the West Florida parishes, the Union Jack of Great Britain sailed on Louisiana winds above British outposts. One in particular, Fort Richmond, was later to be known as Baton Rouge. Its presence on the east bank of the Mississippi was the sorest of thorns in the side of the Spanish.

The Treaty of Paris that had marked the end of the savage French and Indian War gave French Canada to England and French Louisiana to Spain. The terms of the treaty drew a line through the Mississippi River, thus splitting Louisiana. Everything on the east side of the river, Lakes Maurepas and Pontchartrain to Natchez and the Port of Mobile, was given to the British. New Orleans, although also east of the Mississippi, was considered an island, and remained French. According to the rules of treaties, islands can be given to either side.

Unlike the previous banners that flew over Louisiana, the Union Jack was a tricolored flag, blue, white, and red. It bore the symbols of two saints instead of kings: Saints George and Andrew. St. Andrew had been one of the apostles of Christ. St. George had been a knight. Both were Christian martyrs separated in death by 200 years. It was a layered flag designed to show the union of two countries belonging to Great Britain. The flag of England, a white field with the simple red cross of St. George in the foreground, was laid upon the flag of Scotland, a deep blue field with the white X-shaped cross, or saltire, of St. Andrew.

St. George is the patron saint of England. He was believed to be a convert to Christianity who was martyred for his beliefs during the year 303 in the area of the world now known as England.

St. George's cross was adopted by knights during the Crusades. The soldiers of England, encased in armor, reported miraculous stories of victories in battle after praying to St. George for help. By the year 1277, St. George's cross was used as a national insignia in England.

St. Andrew was the brother of Simon Peter, the rock upon whom God had built his Church. Andrew became one of Christ's beloved twelve apostles. He was martyred in the year 60 at Patras, Greece on an X-shaped cross made of two timbers driven into the ground. He was tied to this cross, not nailed. Like his brother Peter who was crucified upside down because he told his executioners he did not deserve to die the same way his Lord had died, Andrew requested the X-shaped cross because he felt undeserving to die the way Christ had.

In the year 370, St. Andrew's bones were carried by ship to what is now Scotland. There, St. Andrew became the patron saint.

In the 1600s after James of Scotland, son of Mary, Queen of Scots, had ascended to the throne of all England, the two kingdoms became one. A flag was needed to show this. Designing a flag under the strict rules of heraldry that would represent the

The British flag

two countries and offend no one would be difficult. But it was accomplished to the happiness of all. The saltire of St. Andrew and the cross of St. George were laid one on top of the other in equal size. A Royal Ordinance dated April 12, 1606 declared the banner the official flag of Great Britain. It was not called the "Union" flag until 1625, at the funeral of King James I. This became the naval flag of the United Kingdom, and was named the Union Jack. A jack is the flag flown by a naval vessel while it is in port.

The Union Jack flew over the West Florida territories and its very closeness to New Orleans, which by 1769 finally came under Spanish rule, was causing much anxiety for the Spanish government. New Orleans would have been quite a prize for the British if they decided to fight for it. And the city's vulnerability would almost assure the English of a victory.

From 1763 to 1776, the British outposts were carefully watched by the Spanish. Then in 1777, a young Spaniard, Bernardo de Gálvez, became governor of Louisiana and the British had their hands full. The British were involved in the Revolutionary War with the Eastern Seaboard colonies. Gálvez secretly gave money to the new American government, and opened Louisiana's ports to American ships. He captured British ships caught carrying illegal cargo in Louisiana waters.

In 1779, Spain declared war on Great Britain. In September of that year, along with Spanish troops, French Louisianians, black men, Indians, and Americans, Gálvez marched to Baton Rouge and attacked the British fort. He used wily military tactics that tricked the British and three hours after his attack began, the Union Jack was lowered from the fort and the red lion and gold castle of Spain were hoisted.

Gálvez' victory that day also forced the British to surrender Natchez. The British were completely driven from Louisiana and their occupation of the east bank of the Mississippi in that territory. It was considered to be the only engagement of the American Revolution on Louisiana soil and it was the last time the British flag ever flew in Louisiana skies.

CHAPTER 5
The French *Trois Couleurs*

THE FLAG OF THE FRENCH REVOLUTION
NOVEMBER 30, 1803—DECEMBER 20, 1803

Although France was a very old country when she once again possessed Louisiana in 1803, her national flag that was hoisted in the Place d'Armes on November 30 represented a very new government. With the lowering of the red and gold Spanish flag that afternoon in New Orleans, Gov. Juan Manuel de Salcedo and the Marquis de Casa Calvo handed Louisiana back to France. The French flag would wave for twenty days, until the Louisiana Purchase was finalized and America would take hold of the territory.

The flag that was raised no longer bore Clovis's fleur-de-lis, nor any symbol of any king. For France had had a revolution, and had erased all reminders of monarchy from anything that was French. The flag was the tricolor, three simple vertical bars of blue, white, and red.

Although some historical versions insist that the original tri-

The French tricolor

color of France had the red bar nearest to the hoist and then switched it with the blue in 1830, the painting of the Louisiana Purchase by nineteenth-century artist Thure de Thulstrup depicts a different story. In that painting, the lowered French flag clearly shows a blue vertical bar nearest the hoist. Other historical versions claim that the blue bar was always nearest the hoist, since the flag's introduction in 1794.

There are also two different stories regarding the flag's designer. It has been written that the Marquis de Lafayette was the original designer, or maybe the artist Jacques Louis David. David belonged to the neoclassical movement of art that was prevalent during the time of the French Revolution. The neoclassical movement took art out of the opulence of the baroque period, and David's paintings done in this style were simple in theme, but powerful in their symmetry and emotion. The simple and strong impact of the flag of France seems to be the work of a neoclassical artist. Its straightforward design and color arrangement have inspired the designs of flags around the world ever since it was adopted during the Convention of 1794 in France.

There are also two recorded stories explaining why the tricolor is blue, white, and red. It was said the blue and red were the official colors of Paris, and the white represented the Bourbon France that had borne the fleur-de-lis. However, most Frenchmen, it is believed, prefer to think the colors come from the red oriflamme of St. Denis, the blue Chape de St. Martin (cope of St. Martin) that Clovis carried, and the white Huguenot (French Protestant) flag. St. Denis, or Dionysius, is the patron saint of France. St. Martin was a bishop who, like Denis, converted many Gauls (French) to Christianity.

The twenty days during which the tricolor flew over Louisiana were peaceful and uneventful. Louisiana had been sold to America in the spring of 1803. On December 20, the beautiful tricolor was lowered and the Stars and Stripes took its official place over the Place d'Armes. There it remained for another fifty-eight years, until 1861, when a revolution of a different kind appeared on Louisiana's horizon and the Stars and Bars flew over a Confederate South.

CHAPTER 6
The American Flag

CONSTELLATIONS
1803-1861

In the year 1803, in a long room of the New Orleans Cabildo called the *Sala Capitular,* the "Council Room," the agreement for the Louisiana Purchase lay on an oblong table covered with emerald-green damask, surrounded by ladder-back chairs placed before a fireplace carved with lions' heads. Outside in the Place d'Armes, the Spanish troops had assembled, and thundering drums accompanied the arrival of the dignitaries at the Cabildo. Eagerly awaiting the ceremony on the balconies of the Pontalba Buildings, ladies in colored, high-waisted Empire gowns of either silk or satin, with plumed bonnets on their heads, stood with elegant men arrayed in gleaming boot leather and fine broadcloth.

It was December 20 and the day was beautiful and dazzling, one of those mild December days that sometimes choose to visit Louisiana near Christmastime. The sunlight, shining on the Pontalba Buildings surrounding the Place d'Armes, turned their rooftops to platinum. The gutters that the Baroness had insisted be covered with gold leaf glinted in the bright light.

On November 30, 1803, only twenty days earlier, the Cabildo had witnessed the ceremonial transfer of Louisiana back to France, in preparation for the American purchase. But that December morning, as the French, American, and Spanish diplomats sat in the Cabildo and witnessed the signing of the Louisiana Purchase making it American territory, perhaps it might have occurred to one of them that many of the historic events that had shaped America had involved something as ordinary as a quill pen. With a mere feather, Thomas Jefferson had written the Declaration of Independence at age thirty-three in 1776, and had defiantly scrawled his signature across the bottom of it. Now, twenty-seven years later, Mr. Jefferson was partly responsible for the use of still another quill on a document that was going to double the size of the already seventeen states of continental America and change history.

The idea was staggering. The cost of Louisiana had been high—15 million dollars. But that madman, Napoleon, storming through Europe like a cyclone, had persuaded Spain to return Louisiana to France, and Jefferson was afraid Napoleon had ideas of controlling North America as well as much of Europe. The influence of another European tyrant in the colonies would be too much to bear, so Jefferson paid the price and acquired Louisiana in the name of America.

Outside in the Place d'Armes, the tricolor of France that had been hoisted for twenty days still flew—but not for long. The flag that had evolved from the first banner of the American Revolution would take its place. The American flag waiting to fly over the Place d'Armes had fifteen stars and fifteen stripes. Vermont and Kentucky had joined the original thirteen states. On January 15, 1794, the American Congress had decreed that the flag would have fifteen stripes with fifteen stars effective May 1, 1795. So much had happened in so short a time to the new nation, and her flag clearly showed this.

The American flag at the time of the Louisiana Purchase

The Flag of the United American Colonies

The Flag of the United American Colonies, first flown in 1769 in Boston by the Sons of Liberty, consisted of thirteen red and white stripes that represented each colony. It was a simple, striking flag that looked like peppermint candy. On the day a most hated Englishman, Sir Francis Bernard, governor of the Massachusetts Bay Colony, was ordered home to England, the Flag of the United American Colonies first flew.

But the flag that holds the official place as the ancestor of the American flag was called the Grand Union flag, or the Cambridge flag. The British Union Jack appeared in the canton on a red-and-white striped field. The striped field was nearly identical to the Flag of the United American Colonies.

The colonists who were protesting much of Great Britain's bad treatment had not yet thought of breaking away as a separate country, nor of designing a new nation's flag. When George Washington surveyed his troops on Prospect Hill near Cambridge from his horse on the icy morning of January 1, 1776, the Grand Union flag was flying over his headquarters. Those who were loyal to Great Britain believed that Washington flew the Grand Union flag to show that he and his rebel troops had seen the error of their ways and were returning to the British fold. But Washington and his Continental Army fiercely drove the British out of Boston a short time later.

Still, in July 1776, when the Declaration of Independence was read, the Grand Union flag was hoisted to signify the United States. And the sight of the Union Jack became intolerable to the new Americans. A new flag was demanded.

Legend tells the story of George Washington visiting a seamstress, Mistress Elizabeth Ross of Philadelphia, with a pencil sketch of the new American flag he had designed, and hiring that lady to make the first flag. Although Washington supposedly told her he wanted a flag made out of red for courage, white for purity, and blue for steadfastness, and although Betsy Ross made naval flags for some of the American officers, there is no written record of her being hired in an official capacity to sew the new flag. The legend began when her grandson, William J. Canby, addressed the Historical Society of Pennsylvania in 1870 and stated that his grandmother had made the first flag. It was a story supposedly handed down from Betsy Ross to her children and grandchildren. The version about her helping Washington design the flag as well as sew it became a popular and accepted belief during the late nineteenth century. However, official records of the Continental Congress point in a different direction—to the true designer of the flag.

Correspondence to the Board of Admiralty, which was forwarded to Congress in 1781, shows one Francis Hopkinson asking for payment for his services for designing the new American flag. A congressional delegate from New Jersey who had signed the Declaration of Independence, and a member of the Naval Board, he had begun to design the flag of the new America, probably to use as a naval flag at first. Keeping the red-and-white striped field of the thirteen colonies, he replaced the Union Jack canton with one containing thirteen stars on a navy-blue background. His choice of stars for the design came from a uniquely personal experience associated with the war.

Hopkinson's family coat of arms contained three stars. During the Revolutionary War, a German soldier fighting for the

British stole a book from Hopkinson's home. On the inside of the front cover, Hopkinson had placed a bookplate with his family coat of arms. Not long after it had been stolen, the book was given to a Philadelphian, who returned it to its rightful owner.

It is presumed that the return of the stars on his coat of arms on the book stolen by an enemy of America moved Hopkinson greatly. It seemed to symbolize the return of the American ideal and to foretell of its success. It is believed that Hopkinson used the stars from his bookplate to complete the design of the American flag.

Six months later, the first Flag Act of June 14, 1777 was passed by the Continental Congress: "Resolved: That the flag of the United States be thirteen stripes, alternate red and white; that the union be thirteen stars, white in a blue field, representing a new constellation." Exact placement of that constellation was never actually described.

Although Hopkinson and Congress went back and forth regarding payment for his services in the years that followed, two things are apparent: the Journals of Congress clearly show he had designed the flag, but they never agreed that he should be paid for it because "he had not been the only one consulted" on the matter. Some of the flags used during the war placed Hopkinson's stars in a circle or ellipse. Other flags had them either in rows, or placed twelve stars in an ellipse with the thirteenth in the center.

The thirteen stripes represent the thirteen original colonies that won American independence against all odds in the year 1783—Delaware, Pennsylvania, New Jersey, Georgia, Connecticut, Massachusetts, Maryland, South Carolina, New Hampshire, Virginia, New York, North Carolina, and Rhode Island—with thirteen stars also symbolizing the same colonies. By 1803, two more stars had been added to the canton of blue: those of Vermont and Kentucky. Although there were seventeen states in the Union at the time of the Louisiana Purchase, Congress did not pass the additional stars for Tennessee and Ohio until July 4, 1818, the same day it also added the stars of

Louisiana, Indiana, and Mississippi. On this date, Congress also decided to return the number of stripes to the original thirteen. Only stars would be added to the canton each time a new territory became a state.

When President Thomas Jefferson was sworn into office in 1801, he sent Robert Livingston to Napoleon's France as an American minister. Two years later, he sent James Monroe to help Livingston negotiate for the purchase of New Orleans from France. At first Napoleon was hesitant, and then he dropped a bombshell. It would not be reasonable for him to hold onto an area the size of Louisiana while no longer controlling her port of entry, New Orleans. He realized he would never be able to defend the area properly if necessary, because he would have no port. And, privately knowing that he was about to go to war with England again and that he needed the money to finance it, Napoleon coolly offered to sell the entire Louisiana territory to the United States of America.

Although they were shocked, Monroe and Livingston accepted the offer, and paid France 15 million dollars with an additional 5 million dollars to cover the cost of all American shipping claims against France. On May 2, 1803, the treaty transferring Louisiana to America was signed between French and American diplomats in France. The United States Senate ratified the purchase in October of that year.

To own the Louisiana territory was to own the Mississippi River. The Mississippi and its tributaries formed one of the most vast networks of waterways found in the entire world. From its almost trickle-like beginning in northern Minnesota down to the roaring gush of its mouth at the Gulf of Mexico, the Mississippi itself was 2,348 miles long. But combined with two of its tributaries, the Missouri and Ohio rivers, it formed a basin that consisted of 1,244,000 square miles stretching between the Appalachian Mountains to the east and the Rocky Mountains to the west.

Louisiana never had an armed conflict for any country to possess her. But for the third time since the French had first settled her, in less than 150 years, she was once again being transferred to the control of another country. Her people were angered and fearful for their culture. And yet, they were also a little curious. They had adapted many times in the past and would soon discover what it meant to be American.

While the flags of most of the nations that had ruled Louisiana had been designed not to offend any kingdom, the American flag was born clearly to insult and defy one kingdom in particular: Great Britain. The theme of the flag that rang true from the very first was that of unity. In some designs, thirteen stars formed almost a wedding band on a blue canton. Then, as the nation grew, more stars appeared on the blue field, symbols of wishes, dreams, and possibilities. And for the colonies that had united against England yet remained joined to one another, thirteen red and white stripes streamed together side by side.

Some designs of the flag placed three stars in a top row, two in a second, three again, then two, then three. With all designs, the flag cried that the glory of this particular country was her free people. Representing their unified efforts and wishes, Old Glory also seemed to ask that Americans never forget that which is fair and just.

In December 1803, the French tricolor was lowered in the Place d'Armes, and the American flag with its fifteen stars and stripes was raised. When the two flags reached the same level on the flagpole, the banners paused briefly. A cannon shot sounded in tribute and was answered by thundering salvos fired from the forts along the river. The American flag flew in New Orleans and across the Louisiana territory.

The Star-Spangled Banner
By Francis Scott Key, 1814

O say, can you see, by the dawn's early light,
What so proudly we hail'd at the twilight's last gleaming,
Whose broad stripes and bright stars, through the
    perilous fight,

FLAGS OF LOUISIANA

O'er the ramparts we watch'd, were so gallantly
    streaming?
And the rockets' red glare, the bombs bursting in air,
Gave proof through the night that our flag was still there.
O say does that star-spangled banner yet wave
O'er the land of the free and the home of the brave?

CHAPTER 7
The Neutral Strip

NO FLAG AT ALL
1806-1819

In 1803, when the United States took possession of Louisiana, the western boundaries of the territory were uncertain. To the west of Louisiana lay Texas, with hardly any human habitation, wild and stark. And beyond Texas lay Mexico, one of the richest Spanish colonies, filled with gold and silver.

By 1805, diplomatic relations between Spain and the United States were strained. Spurred by rumors that American troops were being trained in Kentucky to invade Mexico, the Spanish government began sending patrols from their Nacogdoches base in Texas as far east as Natchitoches in Louisiana. The rumor was not true, but Spain wanted to keep America out of Mexico as much as possible and was prepared to do battle to prove it.

A border dispute raged. The United States insisted that the western border of Louisiana was the Rio Grande, and went no farther east than the Sabine River. The Spaniards argued hotly that the western border of Louisiana was the Arroyo Hondo, a dry gulch just west of Natchitoches.

By 1806, the argument over the boundary was about to erupt into a war between Spain and the United States. American troops, ordered by Gen. James Wilkinson to travel up the Red River, began mobilizing for war. Unknown to the federal government, this American general was also a mercenary paid by the Spanish government as a spy. Surprisingly, this worked as an advantage that prevented any war between the two countries. Acting as a negotiator, General Wilkinson forged a compromise with a Spanish commander. The product of this compromise was "The Neutral Strip," an area of land that lay between the Sabine River on the west and the Arroyo Hondo on the east.

This strip had no government, no flag, no rules. It became a haven for criminals. Thieves and murderers preyed upon the few settlers who lived there. It became one enormous corral for multitudes of stolen horses.

From time to time, Spanish and American troops alternated in sweeping the land of outlaws, until 1819, when the Adams-Onis Treaty finally placed the boundary between Texas and Louisiana at the Sabine River. However, until Fort Jesup was built in 1822, this strip of land remained a hideout for outlaws. This tradition continued to some degree for a long time even after Fort Jesup was established.

CHAPTER 8
The Flag of West Florida

THE BONNIE BLUE FLAG
SEPTEMBER 1810—DECEMBER 1810

The revered and beloved Bonnie Blue flag of the Confederacy had its beginning in Louisiana, some fifty-one years before Louisiana ever seceded from the Union. Even before Texas adopted it in 1836 to signify its independence from Mexico, it had first belonged to a portion of Louisiana known as West Florida.

West Florida had been the part of Louisiana the English had acquired as a result of the Treaty of Paris. It had belonged to Spain and stretched along the muddy Mississippi River from Natchez to Lake Pontchartrain, and from the Mississippi River to the Apalachicola River across the glittering Gulf Coast. The only section in this area that remained Spanish was the Isle of Orleans, flanked by Bayou Manchac and those three lakes that marched in progression to the Gulf of Mexico: Maurepas, Pontchartrain, and Borgne. After the exploits of Louisiana governor Bernardo de Gálvez took West Florida from the British during the Revolutionary War, West Florida again came under Spanish rule.

Many English-speaking colonists had been populating West Florida during the years of British occupation, long before the Louisiana Purchase. A large group of them who sympathized with the Americans during the Revolutionary War asked for sanctuary in Spanish-held Louisiana and began moving into the Mississippi River valley, away from the British. They were mostly Protestant by faith. During the time of the Revolutionary War, the Catholic Spanish government in Louisiana did not persecute them.

By the time of the Louisiana Purchase in 1803, West Florida was once again the fuel for a dispute. Spain had briefly ceded Louisiana back to France as part of the transfer of the territory to the United States. Spain and France argued hotly over which country was going to keep West Florida. Spain stubbornly insisted West Florida was hers and kept possession of her. The boundaries of Louisiana had never been clearly drawn, even by the time the Louisiana Purchase was signed, and the American government left things alone for the time being.

Now the West Floridians, because of their own leanings for liberty, bitterly resented having to remain under Spanish rule. They were angered that the American government failed to annex their territory. In 1804, the Kemper brothers (three men with biblical first names: Reuben, Nathan, and Samuel) led an unsuccessful revolt for West Florida.

During the next six years, the residents of West Florida, so steeped in traditional English culture and so American in their sympathies, no doubt felt more than a little betrayed by the government they had been so loyal to, and equally out of place in the Catholic realm of Spain. They tried to preserve their own precious English culture within the rules of Spanish government. In 1810, the leaders of West Florida began meeting near Bayou Sara, near present-day St. Francisville. They wanted proper representation in the Spanish government, allowing them constitutional rights.

Not so very far away to the southeast, the Spanish commandant of Baton Rouge learned of this plan. When he met with the West Florida leaders, he smiled in their faces and told them how much he supported their ideas. Secretly, he sent a message to the Spanish governor at Pensacola, Don Vicente Folch, asking for troops to smash a revolution that was brewing against Spain.

A later message was intercepted by the West Floridians, and the governor's treachery was exposed. They were outraged. What began as a civilized and peaceful effort to acquire more rights flamed into an armed rebellion.

On a Saturday morning, September 21, 1810, Maj. Isaac Johnson and his mounted troops made their way to the provincial capital of Baton Rouge. The color sergeant at the head of the

The flag of West Florida (Bonnie Blue flag)

column carried the handiwork that one Mrs. Melissa Johnson had sewn together a few days earlier. It was a graceful blue flag moving to the rhythm of the march and the wind. Striking in its simplicity, the banner displayed one large, five-pointed, white star centered on a deep-blue field. It was the Bonnie Blue flag, flag of the new Republic of West Florida. If America did not want them, and Spain did not wish to compromise, they would govern themselves.

This band joined other West Florida troops, which united under the command of Col. Philemon Thomas. They totaled seventy. But luck favored them in the form of a local settler and the fort's cows. The settler showed the West Florida band an unguarded route into the fort—the same route taken each day by the soldiers' cows as they wandered into pasture to graze and returned after a long day in the outdoors to be milked.

When the West Floridians suddenly appeared inside the fort via the cow route, the Spanish soldiers soon surrendered. Two Spaniards died, but there was no West Floridian loss of life. The treacherous governor was imprisoned, and on September 23, 1810, the lone star on the simple Bonnie Blue flag replaced the dramatic red and gold flag of Spain over Fort Baton Rouge. John Rhea, president of the West Florida Convention, signed a declaration of independence on September 26, 1810, and the faithful blue flag flew over the new republic.

The citizens of West Florida adopted a constitution for an independent republic. John Rhea wrote to President James Madison expressing the desire for annexation to America. Before the official letter from Rhea had ever arrived, President Madison heard about the small revolt and ordered American governor William C. C. Claiborne to take possession of the tiny Republic of West Florida. Claiborne hastened to obey.

On October 27, 1810, President Madison declared West Florida to be under the jurisdiction of the governor of Louisiana. West Florida, under American possession, became the parish of Feliciana. Claiborne then divided this land into the parishes of East Baton Rouge, Feliciana, St. Helena, and St. Tammany. On December 10, 1810, the Stars and Stripes were raised over Baton Rouge, and the Bonnie Blue flag was lowered and passed into legend.

The story of the West Florida revolt and its lone star flag captured the imagination of Southerners and became part of Southern tradition. Texas adopted it as a flag of independence in 1836, replacing the one white star with a yellow one, thus giving Texas its nickname, the "Lone Star State." It was also adopted by Mississippi in 1861 for a very brief period.

Although it was never ratified by the Confederate Congress as the official flag of state, it was ratified in the hearts of the people of the Southland as their official flag of emotion. When the song "The Bonnie Blue Flag" was first performed in New Orleans in 1861, it was met with riotous, thunderous approval. The song's popularity helped to spread the romantic lore of the flag.

Back in 1810, however, when the small group of West Floridians were told by Governor Claiborne that they had to become Americans and dissolve their republic, they gave in peacefully. All they had every really wanted from the beginning was just to be American.

The Bonnie Blue Flag
By Harry Macarthy

We are a band of brothers, and native to the soil,
Fighting for our liberty with treasure, blood, and toil;
And when our rights were threaten'd,
The cry rose near and far,
Hurrah for the Bonnie Blue flag
That bears a single star!

CHORUS:
Hurrah, hurrah for Southern rights, hurrah!
Hurrah for the Bonnie Blue flag
That bears a single star!

As long as the Union was faithful to her trust,
Like friends and like brethren, kind were we and just;
But now when Northern treachery attempts our right to mar
We hoist on high the Bonnie Blue flag that bears a single star.

CHORUS

First, gallant South Carolina nobly made the stand;
Then came Alabama, who took her by the hand;
Next, quickly Mississippi, Georgia, and Florida,
All rais'd on high the Bonnie Blue flag that bears a single star.

CHORUS

Ye mean of valor, gather round the Banner of the Right.
Texas and fair Louisiana, join us in the fight;
Davis, our loved president, and Stephens, stateman rare,
Now rally 'round the Bonnie Blue flag that bears a single star.

CHORUS

And here's to brave Virginia! The Old Dominion State
With the young Confederacy at length has link'd her fate;
Impell'd by her example, now other state prepare
To hoist on high the Bonnie Blue flag that bears a single star.

CHORUS

Then cheer, boys, raise the joyous shout,
For Arkansas and North Carolina now have both gone out;

And let another rousing cheer for Tennessee be given.
The single star of the Bonnie Blue flag has grown to be eleven.

CHORUS

Then here's to our Confederacy, strong we are and brave,
Like patriots of old, we'll fight our heritage to save;
And rather than submit to shame, to die we would prefer,
So cheer for the Bonnie Blue flag that bears a single star.

Hurrah, hurrah for Southern rights, hurrah!
Hurrah! For the Bonnie Blue flag has gain'd th'eleventh star!

CHAPTER 9
The National Flag of Louisiana

A NEW ALLEGIANCE
1861

The United States grew rapidly in the nineteenth century, but before too long, the "Union" began to break apart. The Civil War was on the horizon. Louisiana had a large number of pro-Union citizens, but there were slightly more citizens favoring secession. While many people insisted secession could be achieved peacefully, they were largely hollered down. Before Louisiana could officially secede from the Union in early 1861, Gov. Thomas Overton Moore seized most of the federal property in the state: the U.S. arsenal and barracks at Baton Rouge; Forts Jackson and St. Philip, just below New Orleans; and Fort Pike, the U.S. barracks near New Orleans.

Governor Moore's actions just about sealed Louisiana's fate before any secession convention could be held. On January 26, 1861, Louisiana divorced itself from the United States of America. In February in Montgomery, Alabama, Louisiana delegates joined representatives from seven other states and formed the Confederate States of America.

The people voting for secession in 1860 and 1861 did not consider it illegal. No state had been forced into the Union, and any state whose citizens did not wish to become part of the Union were free to do as they pleased. Slavery was only one issue. It was not the main reason why the North and South went to war. The North wanted to preserve the Union—and therefore its power. Also, the wealth of the Southern states greatly contributed to the United States economy. The North was not eager to let them go.

While some Northerners were crying for the freedom of all men, others in the Union army bitterly complained about risking their lives over black men. Some abolitionists were more

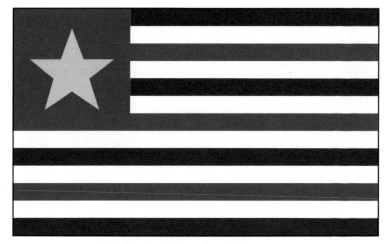

The National Flag of Louisiana

violent than secessionists. An American tragedy was unfold-ing, one side as much to blame and as intolerant as the other.

The convention in Montgomery ratified a new constitution that was very similar to the American Constitution. They thought about naming their new government the "Republic of Washington" or the "Federal Republic of America," but decided on the "Confederate States of America." They established a pro-visional government at first and elected Jefferson Davis as their first and only president.

Louisiana, along with the other states who seceded from the Union, found herself in need of a new state flag. Her people left the Union in anger, but they found it difficult to give up Old Glory, the Stars and Stripes. They loved their country very much—it was her political philosophies that infuriated them.

They adopted a flag that combined their love of America with their pride in Louisiana's past. Like the Star-Spangled Banner, the flag of Confederate Louisiana had thirteen stripes. The colors of the stripes were not taken from the American flag. Instead they came from the tricolored flag of Louisiana's mother country, the red, white, and blue of France.

The flag of Confederate Louisiana also had a canton, and

again the colors were borrowed from Louisiana's past. Upon a red field was placed a large, single, golden star, reflecting the time Louisiana was Spanish. The lone star gave tribute to the courageous little Republic of West Florida, who had triumphed briefly over Spain for independence in Louisiana.

The red and gold flag, with its fiery colors tempered by the cool blue and white stripes, was adopted by Louisiana as its official banner on February 12, 1861. This was just two months before the opening shot of the American Civil War was ever fired at Fort Sumter by Louisiana general P. G. T. Beauregard. It was called the National Flag of Louisiana.

The flag was hoisted over City Hall in New Orleans and other parts of the state, and indicated to everyone that Louisiana had proudly defied the government of the United States.

CHAPTER 10
The Flag of the Confederacy

STARS AND BARS
1861-1865

The Provisional Congress of the Confederate States of America soon formed a Committee on Flag and Seal. It was time to create one flag to represent all of the Confederate states, just as the Stars and Stripes represented the Union. The committee's chairman, William Porcher Miles, was a South Carolinian. His committee received countless designs from people all over the United States, even from states who still belonged to the Union.

Abraham Lincoln was to be inaugurated on March 4, 1861, and the Provisional Congress had set that date for choosing the new Confederate flag. They wished to fly the flag on that day as a show of defiance against Mr. Lincoln. On the morning of

A rejected design for the flag of the Confederacy,
now referred to as the "Confederate flag"

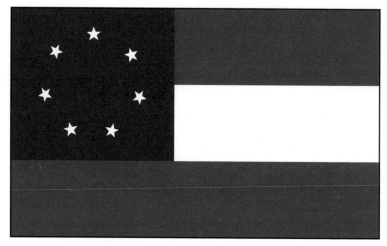

The "Stars and Bars": flag of the Confederacy

March 4, after considering hundreds of designs, the committee presented four flags to Congress for final choice. They were large models of flags, made of cambric (fine linen), and were hung on the walls of the congressional chamber like medieval banners in the halls of kings.

One of the patterns that was rejected went on to become the prototype for the battle flag of the Army of Northern Virginia and then of Tennessee, and today is called the Confederate flag. The red field with the star-studded blue saltire of St. Andrew so apparent today, and so argued about, was not the official flag of the Confederate States selected in Montgomery that day. It was a runner-up.

The flag that was chosen resembled the American flag, and in the first Battle of Bull Run at the beginning of the war would cause great confusion among the soldiers of both sides. It bore a field of scarlet, with a white horizontal space extending through the center of the scarlet. The width of the white space was the same width as the red spaces above and beneath it. In the upper left-hand corner, a union of blue extended down through the white space and stopped at the red below. A circle of seven white stars in the blue union symbolized the seven states of the Confederacy. Through the short life of the Confederacy, as more states seceded, the amount of stars on the union grew. This flag was called the "Stars and Bars."

Exactly who designed the flag has been a subject of furious debate since the Civil War. Strong evidence points equally to two gentlemen, Nicolla Marshall, a German artist, and Orren Randolph Smith from North Carolina. For years, groups of people fought for Mr. Smith or Mr. Marshall to receive sole credit. By 1986, however, enough evidence and enough experts agreed that both men can be given credit for designing the "Stars and Bars" of Dixie.

Their flag design adopted, the Confederate officials scurried to find seamstresses who could sew a suitable flag in time for them to raise it on Mr. Lincoln's hated Inauguration Day. As Chairman Miles expressed it, "thanks to fair and nimble fingers," a flag was sewn within two hours after Congress had chosen it. The flag was made of wool and Miss Letitia Christian Tyler, granddaughter of former president John Tyler, raised the first Confederate flag over the Montgomery capitol building. The Stars and Bars began flying almost immediately over much of the South, even in states that had not seceded but had Southern sympathies. In Louisiana it flew alongside the National Flag of Louisiana. And it was very much in evidence when Louisiana general P. G. T. Beauregard fired on Union troops at Fort Sumter in April 1861.

Beauregard and fellow Louisianian Francis Nicholls served in the grand Army of Northern Virginia, which boasted a stellar cast: Robert E. Lee, Stonewall, J. E. B. Stuart, James Longstreet. In the first broiling summer of the war, in the first major battle at Manassas, Virginia, near the creek called Bull Run, confusion reigned for Union and Confederate armies alike. There was no uniformity of clothing to properly identify each side. And for the Army of Northern Virginia, the similarity of the new Confederate flag to Old Glory nearly cost them the battle.

Although the Confederate army soundly beat the Yankees, General Beauregard wanted a solution to the flag problem immediately. The Army of Northern Virginia was commanded overall by Gen. Joseph E. Johnston, who suggested that the army troops should use their state flags for proper identification, but only the Virginia troops were in a position to comply. Beauregard communicated with Congressman Miles and asked that the Confederate flag be changed.

Although Miles understood the problem, he knew Congress would not approve of the idea and said so to the Louisiana general. As an alternative, Miles suggested that the Army adopt a design for its own battle flag. Remembering the design he had himself favored when the Confederate leaders were choosing a new standard, he offered this idea: the blue cross of St. Andrew, studded with stars for the Confederate states, waving on a brilliant red background.

Both Beauregard and Johnston approved of the flag, with Johnston requiring that its shape be square for use in battles. Hettie, Jennie, and Constance Carey sewed three prototypes for

The "Southern Cross": battle flag
of the Army of Northern Virginia

the generals' consideration. In September 1861, the quarter-masters of the army were told to have the flags produced and issued to the troops.

By November, the flag that would be known as the "Southern Cross" was flown by the Army of Northern Virginia. It bore on its blue St. Andrew's cross twelve stars—eleven for the Confederate states and one for Missouri, a state that had seceded but had not yet been admitted to the new "union." It was made of silk and trimmed in gold, but in time, fine English wool bunting proved a more durable fabric to weather the rigors of the elements and war, and the gold trim would be replaced with orange.

Today there are ongoing efforts to remove any of these "Confederate flags" from public display. It is ironic that there are strong objections to a banner that was not the official Confederate flag and was never used as a symbol of racism during this most bloody conflict. The majority of Southerners fighting the war were poor men and only 10 percent of the army owned slaves. The Emancipation Proclamation freeing the slaves was not issued until 1863, and was a political move by Mr. Lincoln. It only freed the slaves living in the states that had actually seceded from the Union. It also helped prevent Queen Victoria of England from giving financial support to the Southern army. Although she believed in the Southern cause of states' rights, she could not uphold slavery and withheld aid from the Confederates.

In the late 1840s Robert E. Lee, a very Christian man who abhorred slavery, freed his four slaves. In 1862, while fighting the Civil War, he freed all of the slaves his wife had inherited from her father. On the other hand, Union general Ulysses S. Grant, who fought under Old Glory, never liberated the slaves he had acquired through marriage, although he was "fighting against slavery."

There weren't many Confederate soldiers fighting to preserve the institution of slavery. The planter class, who owned the majority of slaves, was in the minority. Instead, the Confederates were fighting for the right of self-government. Many realized, along with their Northern brothers, that slavery was an immoral and antiquated system that had no future. They only wanted to resolve it within the guidelines of states' rights. Many Southerners believed they were fighting the second American Revolution and the federal government was as much a tyrant as King George. The Confederate flag was not a symbol of proslavery and white supremacy, but of states' rights.

In the months after secession, the parishes of Louisiana began forming their own military brigades. And like Napoleon, who realized he could not control the Louisiana territory unless he controlled New Orleans, the federal government immediately set its sights on the Crescent City. By the time the Civil War began, New Orleans was the largest city in the South and the fifth largest city in the entire nation.

The Yankees wanted to capture the Mississippi, starting at the mouth of the river, and then through to New Orleans, working their way up. At the same time, they could work their way down the river from Cairo, Illinois, conquering from two directions, meeting at some triumphant point. This was called the "Anaconda" plan. The anaconda is a large South American boa constrictor that crushes its prey.

If New Orleans were captured, the vital port city that fed the Confederacy would be crippled. If Vicksburg, high on bluffs and called the "Gibraltar of the Mississippi," could be captured, then so would the Mississippi River, and the entire Confederacy would be cut in two. The anaconda would have devoured its prey.

On April 19, 1861, Lincoln called for a massive naval blockade of all states that had seceded. Gunboats were placed on the Mississippi at Cairo and in the Gulf of Mexico. Four ships began patrolling the mouth of the Mississippi River just below New Orleans.

By 1862, Louisiana's sons had seen Manassas in Virginia and Shiloh in Tennessee. New Orleanians got a full taste of the sheer horror of war when trainloads of dead and wounded began pouring into their city after the bloodbath of Shiloh. Adding to their worries was the presence of a Union fleet on Ship Island.

Forts St. Philip and Jackson protected the Crescent City near the Gulf of Mexico. The Confederates, in further defense of the city, had stretched a long chain across the river, but the amount of debris floating on the Mississippi was high that year and the chain broke. So another barrier was constructed just below the two forts. Farther upriver, a large number of rafts and barges piled twenty feet high with dry tinder soaked in tar and kerosene were moored on either shore. The rafts and barges would be ignited the minute any Yankees appeared, and freed so they could burn the wooden ships in the enemy fleet.

Despite all their preparation, the Confederates were taken off guard on the morning of April 18 when the Union fleet fired on the forts. The ships had been hidden around a bend and camouflaged. The Confederate guns snarled back.

For the next four days, the Union fleet was unable to pass the Confederate forts. So under cover of night, the Yankees sliced through the chained barrier, taking Confederate fire all the while. The Union ships advanced, only to meet the Confederate rafts now set on fire.

The Yankees fought the fire. In one hour and ten minutes, it was over. The Union ships had passed the forts, and were steaming their way towards New Orleans.

By the time the sun had risen on the morning of April 24, word had reached New Orleans that Union ships had passed the two forts that had been the Crescent City's only defense. Panic hit the city. Cotton and warehouses went up in smoke so that the enemy would find nothing valuable. By the following morning, the streets were wild with looters and more buildings were set on fire.

The 32,000 soldiers stationed in the city began evacuation. A drenching April rain that had begun the night before was still pouring on New Orleans. The banks of the Mississippi were overflowing.

From the levees, the Union ships could be seen in the distance as they engaged the Confederates at Chalmette for a brief time. The Yankees slid past Chalmette. From the top of the masts hung the Stars and Stripes, growing larger and larger as the ships neared New Orleans and docked.

On April 26, 1862, two federal naval officers raised the United States flag over the Mint. A professional gambler named William Mumford climbed up the flagpole and tore the Stars and Stripes down. He hurled it into the mob, which quickly destroyed it. Mr. Mumford had unknowingly signed his own death warrant. He was hanged for this act by the United States on June 7.

The Stars and Bars disappeared from the city and much of the Mississippi River as the Union navy conquered Baton Rouge and crept up towards Vicksburg. Shreveport was the last holdout against surrender. Gen. Edmund Kirby Smith did not lower the Confederate flag there until June 5, 1865. But for the duration of the Civil War, the western half of Louisiana still flew the Stars and Bars and the National Flag of Louisiana. The Union army never completely conquered the state.

In 1865, the war ended. Over half a million lives had been lost in total from either side. The lives of the survivors had been shattered. Northern families were broken up by death as well as Southern families. Reconstruction of the South was under way.

Caught somewhere in the middle were the slaves, now freedmen. Sadly, the North, having won the war, abandoned them to their own devices. It didn't matter that they were poverty-stricken just as long as they were no longer slaves.

The Stars and Bars had flared and died. The defiant South was absorbed back into the Union.

CHAPTER 11
The State Flag

SACRIFICIAL LOVE
1912-

The story of the state flag of Louisiana begins with the state's seal, which reaches back to the year of 1812. On April 30 of that year, the boundary lines were drawn that designated the new state of Louisiana and she was admitted to the Union. And Louisiana now had a state legislature.

Flags with a large mother pelican and her young began appearing throughout the state in 1812. The pelican flag accompanied the delegates to the Confederate Assembly of 1861, and for a brief period of time *was* the Louisiana Confederate flag until the lone star flag in the colors of France and Spain replaced her in February of 1861. June 23, 1813 records clearly show an emblem with a pelican, the word *Justice* and a pair of scales, and then the phrase *Union and Confidence*. It is believed that Governor Claiborne may have used these symbols before any official act called for a state seal.

However, now that she was a state, Louisiana was in need of an official state seal. On December 23, 1813, the legislature passed Act No. 5, which decreed, "The State Government shall be provided with a public seal, with such device and inscription as the Governor may direct." The first seal of the State of Louisiana showed a nest teeming with a dozen, perhaps more, young pelican birds. As time and enlightenment progressed, this was changed to three young nesting pelicans. By the laws of nature, a pelican only has three young.

In 1864, after Henry Watkins Allen was elected, a new seal was made. Governor Allen was a Confederate brigadier general. Severely wounded in the battle of Baton Rouge, he had to walk on crutches for the rest of his life. When he was elected governor, the Civil War was still being fought, and his administration covered the areas of the state that still remained Confederate.

He did his best to ease the horrid conditions the war had brought about in Louisiana. With most of the state's cotton almost rotting in storage because of the Union blockades and the capture of the Mississippi, Allen established cotton trade with Mexico using land routes through Texas. This brought arms and civilian products into the state.

At Mount Lebanon University, he established a laboratory that manufactured medicines that were in desperate short supply. In the name of the state, Mr. Allen purchased an iron-ore deposit in Texas. He created jobs by building a foundry in Shreveport, where the metal obtained from the deposit could be worked.

Pensions were paid to war widows and war orphans, and state stores were established so that the people receiving state money could also buy products in order to live. It is fitting that for his seal he still chose the pelican. In his seal, the protective mother pelican hovered over her young in the nest, accompanied by the motto *Justice, Union and Confidence* and a pair of scales.

When Gov. J. Madison Wells was elected, he adopted a seal closely resembling Governor Allen's. But in opposition to natural law, four pelican young were in the nest. The head of the mother pelican was reversed. Not long after his administration ended, the motto on the state seal was changed to *Union, Justice and Confidence*. In 1870, the scales were left off of the seal.

The pelican on the state flag and the state seal is the brown pelican, a bird whose nesting path reaches from South Carolina to Brazil. Known for their famous large bills, the birds almost always seem to be smiling. The lower part of their bills contain a large pouch that can be greatly extended. Their favorite food is fish and they nest close to water. They catch their meals by scooping pouches full of salt water. A pelican that is only one month old can devour five pounds of fresh fish a day.

In 1902, the Great Seal of the State of Louisiana was officially adopted. Gov. W. W. Heard obeyed Section 3471 of the Revised Statutes, which ordered an official adoption of a state seal. It was a pelican with her head turned to the left, wings spread over a nest holding her three young. Encircling her head are the words

The state flag

Union and Justice. Beneath the nest is the word *Confidence.*

The mother pelican is in the act of tearing her breast to feed her young. She represents the state; the pelican young who gaze up at her with such trust represent the people of Louisiana— her children. Natural history does not support this old legend that a pelican will tear her own breast to feed her young, but the image has long been used to symbolize sacrifical love. Governor Claiborne seemed to believe this was a trait of pelicans, which was one of the reasons why he chose the bird for the seal so long ago.

A drawing of a pelican was found by H. L. Favrot in an old Catholic prayer book. The prayer book belonged to a member of that long-ago first legislature of 1813. The picture in the prayer book shows the pelican as a symbol of self-sacrifice. Perhaps this was shown to Mr. Claiborne, governor of Catholic Louisiana, who was inspired enough by the legend to give the pelican an exalted place in the state seal.

FLAGS OF LOUISIANA

On July 1, 1912, 100 years after the pelican made its first appearance as a state symbol, a flag to represent Louisiana was adopted. Its field is solid blue, and the state seal is reproduced in gold and white. A banner beneath the nest of clamoring young pelicans reads, *Union, Justice and Confidence.* It is a flag that conveys that Louisiana is a family united in justice and is confident and secure in that knowledge.

PART II

FLAGS OF LOUISIANA'S
PARISHES AND CITIES

CHAPTER 12
Parish Flags

ACADIANA

The flag of Acadiana waves over twenty-two parishes in Louisiana, or, as Longfellow called it in his epic poem, "Evangeline," the "Eden of Louisiana." Longfellow's tragic love story of Gabriel and Evangeline, two Acadians who lost one another when they were expelled from Nova Scotia, was taken from real life—with some liberties. Louis Pierre Arceneaux and Emmeline Labiche, two lovers betrothed to one another and separated by the exile, eventually found one another years later in St. Martinville, Louisiana. Louis was betrothed to another woman and poor Emmeline died from a broken heart. They became Longfellow's Evangeline and Gabriel.

Some years later, one of Louis's descendants, Dr. Thomas J. Arceneaux, decided to design a flag in tribute to the Acadian region. A resident of Lafayette, Dr. Arceneaux was the Dean of Agriculture at the University of Southwestern Louisiana from 1941 to 1973. He had led the French Renaissance movement in Louisiana at the time of the 200th anniversary of the expulsion of the Acadians from Nova Scotia (1755).

His efforts and those of others in the French Renaissance greatly served to restore interest in the Cajun culture and preserve its heritage. Dr. Arceneaux set out to design a flag that would capture the unique essence of the Acadian culture. For inspiration, he turned to her history, back to 1605, long before the Treaty of Utrecht.

In 1605, a large number of French people settled in Nova Scotia, in North America. The colonists named the land Acadie. They were devoutly Catholic and devoutly French, and no doubt the blue flag with the gold fleur-de-lis flew over their province.

They sang and danced to a music rich with rhythm that had

been passed down to them by mouth, generation to generation, since the time of medieval France. The triangle and fiddle were their only instruments at the time.

They had left France during a time when the Virgin Mary, the Blessed Mother of Jesus, was greatly revered. She was the patroness of France. In 1638, all of France's lands were consecrated to Mary. She was given the title "Our Lady of the Assumption."

In 1713, the Treaty of Utrecht awarded the province of Acadie to the English. Terms of the treaty stated that all farmers residing in Acadie could either remain or sell their land and migrate to areas in Canada other than Nova Scotia. What's more, the Acadians were promised, if they chose to remain, they would be free to practice their Catholic religion.

But the governor of Nova Scotia, Francis Nicholson, was afraid a mass exodus of farmers from Acadie would deplete the region's economy. His other concern was that French power might grow in other sections of Canada if he lost the Acadians. He forbade any emigration. The Acadians loved their homes and farms so familiar to them and did not wish to leave.

When the time allotted for the migration to take place had passed, and hardly any Acadians had left, Protestant England insisted that they take a modified oath of allegiance to England. They were still allowed to practice their Catholicism and would not be forced to join the British military to bear arms against France. They were known as the French Neutrals.

Although they proudly maintained their French language and customs, the Acadians were careful to carry out their sworn duty as English subjects. But as the middle of the eighteenth century approached, England became more demanding. England wanted complete allegiance sworn to the Crown, which also included rejection of the Catholic religion. In addition, English law decreed that only a loyal subject of the Crown had the privilege of owning any land.

The Acadians refused to go along with this. In 1749, thousands of Acadian families exiled themselves from Nova Scotia. By 1755, Gov. Charles Lawrence ordered the remaining population to swear allegiance to Great Britain—or else. But the Acadians would not abandon their mother country nor the religion of their souls and consequently all of their lands were confiscated. The farmhouses and churches were burned and the English soldiers forced families onto ships in scenes of exquisite cruelty.

Approximately seven thousand exiles arrived in the American colonies, where they were not warmly received. A large number of the Acadians died on the boats in harbor as they waited for someone to allow them to come ashore and live. Many died in detention camps or wound up in England, France, some of the American colonies, and even the West Indies.

Loving the culture for which they had given up so much, the Acadians turned with hope to French Louisiana. Thousands began migrating there. But by the time they arrived in the mid-1760s Louisiana had been ceded to Spain by France.

The Spanish government welcomed them. After all, the kings of both France and Spain were cousins. Like the Spaniards, the Cajuns were also Catholic and both cultures had felt the extent of the cruelty the English government could inflict on anyone who got in its way. The Spanish government gave them land grants, allowing them to settle in the largely unpopulated Attakapas region.

They came to a primeval land filled with trees covered in moss, the air heavy with moisture. Spain was good to them, and they were free to be French. They embraced the rugged new land that became their home and they prospered in joy.

The area was a mixture of forests, treeless prairies, bayous, and swamps. They named oak-covered ridges that were once ancient beaches on the Gulf of Mexico *chenières*. Their houses were built of the strong, fragrant wood of the cypress tree held together with *bousillage,* a mixture of Spanish moss and mud that acted as insulation between the exterior and interior walls. A high-pitched roof was built for the dual purpose of running off water in the heavy rains and of providing attic space that could also be used as sleeping quarters for the young male family members. This was called a *garçonnière*. A stairway that led

The flag of Acadiana

to the attic was always built on the front porch so that it did not take up any of the precious indoor space of the house, and could be used for front-porch seating as well. And the Acadians combined their fine French provincial cooking heritage with the blend of cultures they discovered in America—Spanish, Indian, and African.

By the time of the American Revolution, the French Acadians in Louisiana considered themselves to be loyal subjects of Spain. Bernardo de Gálvez was governor and Spain declared war on Great Britain. The English were occupying Manchac, Baton Rouge, Mobile, and Pensacola and Gálvez succeeded in driving them out of southern America, something that assisted the American colonies immensely. Fighting with him were many loyal Acadians.

So, in 1965, Dr. Arceneaux designed his flag. The upper portion consists of an angular blue field with three silver fleur-de-lis, to represent the Cajuns' mother country, the kingdom of France. The lower portion is an angular red field with the castle of Castile upon it, in tribute to the kingdom of Spain, which ruled Louisiana, gave safe harbor to the expelled Acadians, and was so kind to them. Stretching in a white triangle nearest the hoist and almost to the center of the flag, a third kingdom is represented.

"For behold I saw a woman clothed with the sun with the moon at her feet and upon her head she wore a crown of twelve stars" (Rev. 12:1). The white field bears a single gold star, symbol of the Virgin Mary. The litany to Mary calls her "Morning Star" and "Star of the Sea." In 1938, Pope Pius XI proclaimed Our Lady of the Assumption to be the patroness of all Acadians, either living in America or anywhere in the world. And so, her star is depicted on the flag.

Note: The twenty-two parishes of Acadiana are: Acadia, Ascension, Assumption, Avoyelles, Calcasieu, Cameron, Evangeline, Iberia, Iberville, Jefferson Davis, Lafayette, Lafourche, Pointe Coupee, St. Charles, St. James, St. John the Baptist, St. Landry, St. Martin, St. Mary, Terrebonne, Vermilion, and West Baton Rouge.

OUACHITA PARISH

On the map of Louisiana, as your eye travels to the northeastern corner of the state, you'll find Ouachita Parish. On its eastern border, Bayou La Fourche snakes and curves around, marking the line between Ouachita and Richland parishes. Dropping through the city of Monroe and running almost through the center of the parish is the Ouachita River.

In 1993, the Ouachita Police Jury announced a contest to design a flag that would do honor to the parish. They promised the community that all parish employees, fire fighters, and policemen would wear the new emblem on their uniforms. The parish flag would take its place of honor beneath the American flag in front of the courthouse.

The contest would be judged by flag-makers from Valley Forge, Pennsylvania, and the designs were to symbolize the parish in a simple, colorful way. Larger writing was encouraged so it could be easily seen when the flag was at full mast. The

The flag of Ouachita Parish

community joined together with enthusiasm and the committee was swamped with many designs.

Ouachita was among the original nineteen parishes of Louisiana. The name comes from the Ouachita Indians, who peopled the area. Indian mounds that belonged to the Indians are found throughout the parish. "Ouachita" means silver water.

It is believed that on his quest to explore the Mississippi River valley, Hernando de Soto reached Ouachita Parish. In 1720, French colonists began settling this northeastern part of Louisiana. The parish was finally incorporated in 1807.

The twin cities of Monroe and West Monroe lie on either side of the Ouachita River. Today, these cities are a crossroads of commerce, having both railway lines and vital highways traveling through them. The towns were settled by people who journeyed from the French missions found along the Mississippi River in Concordia and Catahoula parishes. They were also trading posts for Indians, trappers, and hunters.

In time the settlement was called Fort Miró. But one May evening in 1819, a steamboat named the *James Monroe* docked at the riverbank. All of the citizens rushed to see the steamer named after their president. It was decided at a huge celebration that very evening to change the name of Fort Miró to Monroe.

In 1993, by the time ten finalists had been picked in the flag contest, the judges declared that it had been most difficult to narrow the field, since they had seen countless beautiful flags. On July 3, 1993, the winner was announced. On a white field, the word *Ouachita* was written in enormous red script from the lower left to the upper right. Under the script, on the same diagonal, a wide blue body of water curved through the field, not touching the lettering. On the upper part of the flag, the same pattern of wide, deep-blue water was repeated, and it sailed right through the middle of the enormous *O* of *Ouachita*. Its designers were the fifth-grade reading students of Central Elementary School in Calhoun, Louisiana.

It was a striking, colorful flag that had cleverly achieved the objective of capturing the essence of Ouachita Parish. It almost resembled the primitive art of the Indians who had settled the parish long ago. Additionally, the geography of the parish was illustrated by the wavy lines in the design. The top wave traveling through the *O* symbolized the Ouachita River flowing through the city of Monroe. The lower wave represented Bayou La Fourche, the eastern boundary of Ouachita Parish.

CHAPTER 13
City Flags

ABBEVILLE

In 1843, when the city of Lafayette was still named "Vermilionville," a French priest named Père Antoine Desire Megret traveled to a bluff twenty miles away. The bluff, high as a church's steeple, overlooked the Vermilion River as it lazily meandered to mingle with the Gulf of Mexico. Père Megret had wandered like any pilgrim, searching for the perfect spot where he could begin to accomplish his mission—the founding of a house of God. On that day in 1843, standing somewhere between the sky and the river, that most pious man knew his search was over.

He purchased the surrounding land for $900 from Joseph LeBlanc and called the area "La Chapelle," which is French for "chapel." Père Megret changed its name a little later to "Abbeville" after his hometown in France. "Abbeville" means "priest town."

Abbeville was patterned after the towns of France, and has two town squares. It was appropriately settled by the French-speaking Acadians, the Cajuns whose ancestors had been expelled from Nova Scotia nearly a century before. They had made their stand against the English government and refused to give up Catholicism. They had lost everything because of it. A hundred years later, their ancestors began a life in Catholic "Priest Town."

The settlement grew and was officially chartered as a town in 1850. Père Megret administered to his new town's spiritual and physical needs. A graceful, charming little city began to emerge, and as time went by, the Old French and Acadian cultures were enriched by additional races and creeds. Abbeville became the parish seat of Vermilion Parish, which extends from

ABBEVILLE

POUR DIEU ET LA PATRIE

1850

The flag of Abbeville

the salty Gulf of Mexico deep into the murky swamps of Louisiana. The parish became the largest rice producer in the state, and ranked high in beef production.

On July 21, 1958, over a century after Père Megret began La Chapelle, the city council adopted its first official city flag. Designed by a local optometrist, Dr. S. J. LaBorde, the flag made its first public appearance on September 5, 1958. Although it was 1958, and Elvis Presley, the Everly Brothers, and Fats Domino had the nation jolting to rock 'n' roll, and in movie houses people were being jolted out of their seats by 3-D films, the flag revealed by the Abbeville City Council looked as if it had been pulled from the halls of medieval kings.

It was a beautiful red flag, the color chosen in tribute to the parish, Vermilion. Upon this brilliant red was a snow-white shield, shaped in a symbolic form that stood for courage, something of which Père Megret had plenty. The choice for a white shield was twofold: it represented Père Megret's purity of motive for founding Abbeville, and also recalled the old Lily Flag of Bourbon France, upon which had flown the three fleur-de-lis. A blue diagonal stripe through the center of the shield symbolized the priest's courage and the courage of the Cajuns who had stood up against religious persecution, braved life in a strange land, and turned it into a celebration. A plain brown cross in the upper part of the shield referred to the religious foundation of the town. The simplicity of the crucifix perhaps suggests that faith needs no decoration, and is indeed a reward unto itself. A single golden fleur-de-lis of Bourbon France is found in the lower part of the shield, once again recalling the time when Louisiana was the daughter of France.

Above and below the shield it says *Abbeville* and *1850*, the year she was finally recognized as a town. A white streamer below the shield bears the French words *Pour Dieu et la Patrie*, meaning "For God and Country." Père Megret understood the meaning of this very well.

NEW IBERIA

The origins of the flag of New Iberia, as well as the name of its designer, are a bit obscure. Yet the flag does exist, and proudly flies over City Hall. It is a quartered flag, the white and emerald-green quarters placed diagonally from one another. The words *New Iberia* appear in the white quarter nearest the hoist in green lettering. The word *Louisiana* appears in the same green lettering on the lower white quarter.

An emblem at the center of the field, in the shape of a shield, is also quartered in diagonal green and white, the shield edged in yellow-gold. Above the shield is a gold crown that bears the inscription *1779* in white. A gold banner surrounds the bottom half of the shield, connecting two green stalks of sugarcane that flank the emblem. The banner reads, in white letters, *Queen City of the Teche.*

New Iberia lies on the Old Spanish Trail, which is now Highway 182. This trail stretched from Florida to San Antonio. New Iberia was first settled in 1779 by a group of Spaniards and other colonists from the Canary Islands. They were sent to this section of Louisiana, where once lived the Attakapas Indians, the first and only Louisiana cannibals on record, to experiment with the farming of hemp and flax. The fibers of hemp, a tall plant, were used to manufacture rope. Flax was a blue-flowered plant cultivated for fibers that were used in weaving.

The Spanish named their tiny new outpost in Louisiana "New Iberia," after the home they had just left and still loved—the Iberian Peninsula. The town was incorporated in 1836. When Iberia Parish was created in 1868, New Iberia was named the parish seat. The tradition of warmth and graciousness that was begun by its early settlers is carried on in New Iberia to this day, and she is still known as the "Queen City of the Teche."

Bayou Teche runs through New Iberia, and is in the heart of Louisiana's sugarcane belt. The sugarcane plant figures largely on the city's flag. The annual income from sugarcane cultivated in the belt is over 19 million dollars.

The flag of New Iberia

The Teche Country is a mixture of heritages—French, Acadian, and Spanish. French is still fluently spoken in most of the region. The Teche Country is filled with green mystery—ancient giant oaks filled with Spanish moss preside over meandering bayous that teem with fish, migratory birds, and other wildlife creatures.

Symbols that represent the bounty of New Iberia appear in four quarters of the shield on the city flag. The city and the surrounding areas are situated on top of three of the largest salt domes in the world, and this is represented on the flag's shield. The lower white quarter shows salt pouring from a container. Salt mines and plants are common in the area, and are found at Weeks Island, Jefferson Island, and Avery Island. Together they yield 1,500,00 tons of salt yearly—some of the purest salt found in the entire world.

The hot red peppers that are used to make Mr. McIlhenny's world-famous Tabasco sauce at his plant in New Iberia are also given a place of honor on the shield. Although the fiery red peppers are colored white on the flag, three of them appear in the lower green quarter. The recipe for Tabasco sauce uses salt taken directly from the domes found in New Iberia and surrounding areas.

The upper white quarter of the shield shows a green-colored oil rig with two seabirds flying on either side. Offshore oil drilling in the parish produces 16,000,000 barrels of oil a year, thus making Iberia the number-one oil-producing parish in the state.

And finally, the upper green quarter shows a plantation house, probably Shadows-on-the-Teche. The area around New Iberia is jeweled with plantation homes, magnificent reminders of the antebellum period of Louisiana. In the spring, their gardens are filled with regal irises, azaleas, and camellias.

The romance of its history, the sheer poetry of its scenery, and the bustling success of its industry are captured on the flag of New Iberia. It is a region of Louisiana that seems to have achieved a fine balance between the bustling energy of America and the lazy, romantic dreams of the Old South. The flag of New Iberia reflects this remarkable balance.

NEW ORLEANS

As the bicentennial of the founding of New Orleans approached, the people realized they had no official city flag. A contest sponsored by the Citizens' Flag Committee was announced. The best design submitted would be chosen as the flag of New Orleans. Three hundred seventy-nine entries were submitted.

On February 5, 1918, the New Orleans Commission Council adopted the winning flag. It was submitted by Bernard Barry and Gus Couret. The flag consisted of a wide white field edged on top with a crimson stripe and on the bottom of with an electric-blue stripe. In the center of the white field, three gold fleur-de-lis were placed in the shape of a V.

Mr. Barry and Mr. Couret chose white to represent purity of motive, believing that only a government motivated by purity

The flag of New Orleans

and goodness can bring about justice and equality. The crimson stripe symbolizes brotherhood—one blood, united. The blue stripe represents liberty, which comes from a pure government. It is apparent that these two men created a flag with a family theme—the white field for purity was larger than the rest of the flag because purity was the mother of both fraternity and liberty—her red and blue offspring at the top and bottom of the banner. The three gold fleur-de-lis symbolized New Orleans at her birth, when she was founded in the name of France. The two designers thought it significant to place the fleur-de-lis on the white field of purity and democracy—they had symbolically snatched it from the old banner of French kings who had ruled so strongly. Now, the symbol of arrogant kings was placed on the field of triumphant freedom.

Mr. Barry and Mr. Couret chose red, white, and blue because they were the colors of both the United States of America and of France. France had been the mother country of New Orleans; America was now her wise and unselfish stepmother.

The heads of the Flag Committee, W. O. Hart and W. J. Waguespack, presented this design to Mayor Martin Behrman, who accepted it. On February 9, 1918, the flag was raised on the rooftop of City Hall. There it waved with its vivid colors, atop the white Grecian building on St. Charles Street called Gallier Hall.

SHREVEPORT

In 1934, just a year before the centennial celebration to commemorate the founding of Shreveport, the city realized it had no flag. It was the depression. The streets of Shreveport were filled with Ford Model-T cars and Mr. Roosevelt was in the White House. People escaped their worries by going to the movies when they could afford to, or listening to the radio at home when they could not. Communities and farmers banded together during these very hard times and money was scarce. But Shreveport was about to have a birthday. The town had been founded because one man had done the impossible. The citizens wanted to celebrate.

The flag of Shreveport

In the 1830s, Henry Miller Shreve cleared the "Red River Raft"—a massive jam of logs in the river that stretched 160 miles across the state, blocking the waterways and making the northern half of Louisiana inaccessible from the southern half. When the raft was at last cleared, he established a trading post on a bluff in northern Louisiana. This became Shreveport, one of the largest cities in Louisiana.

State legislator Rupert Peyton suggested having a contest to select the best design for the city's new flag. Through various channels and other interested people, including Mr. L. A. Mailhes, the idea reached the Shreveport City Council. The council approved the proposal, formed a committee, and laid the ground rules for the contest. No artists were approached or appointed; instead the contest was open to men, women, and children of all backgrounds and occupations, which also included students. First prize, in addition to the honor of having their handiwork fly above the city for posterity, would be fifty dollars. Designs submitted must be in color and twelve by eighteen inches in dimension.

Members of the Contest Committee who would decide on the city's banner were: Aaron Selber (chairman), Sam B. Bogan, Leonard J. Daniels, Mrs. C. R. Caldwell, Mrs. W. E. Wallace, E. W. Jones, and Mrs. Frank J. Melelon. The committee received large numbers of beautiful designs. All contestants signed agreements transferring ownership of their designs to the city. As the committee began choosing the top designs as finalists, the retail stores of Shreveport proudly displayed them in their windows.

The contest winner was a veteran of World War I named Stewart G. Davis. He was also a local artist. His flag had been chosen by the committee because of its vivid colors, its beauty, and its historical significance. Mr. Davis, as he accepted his fifty-dollar prize, a bounty in those depression days, happily announced his design was "the best piece of work I've ever done."

The background of his flag resembles, except for its colors, the tricolored flag of France in use since the 1790s. The three vertical bars are French blue nearest the hoist, white in the center, and gold last. The blue represents Louisiana under France, the white borrows from the white stripes of the Star-Spangled Banner, and the vivid gold repeats the imperial gold of the flag of Spain.

At the flag's center, on the white bar, Mr. Davis placed a most beautiful design. A shield was formed, crowned by the white pelican to symbolize the State of Louisiana. In the upper right of the shield, on a deep-blue field, eighteen gold stars with five points filled the area. Louisiana was the eighteenth state to enter the Union and Mr. Davis used the stars to signify this. In the center of the shield, a red band runs diagonally across, and serves as a background for three snowy magnolia blossoms, the state flower. They are three in number to represent Shreveport as the regional capital of northern Louisiana, eastern Texas, and southern Arkansas. In the lower left area of the shield, on a

The flag of Slidell

white field, a symbol borrowed from the Henry Miller Shreve family coat of arms appears in dark-blue cones and dots. A wreath of cotton leaves, depicting the main agricultural product of the area, surrounds the bottom of the shield. Beneath this, a white ribbon streamer is inscribed with blue letters that read, *City of Shreveport—1835.*

In 1965, Shreveport refocused attention on Mr. Davis's beautiful flag that captured the spirit and heritage of Mr. Shreve's trading post. Today, it is widely displayed at city functions and festivals.

SLIDELL

If ever you are in an adventuresome mood, and feel like having a rather hair-raising experience, take the train to Slidell from New Orleans, or vice versa. You will be traveling to, or from, the "Ozone Belt," where the freshest air in the world, purified by many pine forests, can be found. In New Orleans, the train will whip and clack past graveyards where the quiet people sleep. It will fly past backyards where the not-so-quiet children play, who wave as you watch them from the train window.

The train will follow the interstate for a while and some cars may try to race it. Then it will pass the old moss-covered oaks of City Park, and wind its way past weather-beaten fishing camps on stilts above the water. Either before or after New Orleans, depending upon which direction you're coming from, you must, at some point, experience the lake from the train.

The train bridge that connects the north shore with the south is a long, skinny affair with no guard railing, and rises just a few feet above the surface of Lake Pontchartrain. Looking from the window, you can't see the tracks at all—only the water, which is colored by the whimsy of the sky on any given day. You are so close to the lake you can see tiny bubbles swirling with the water and miniscule schools of fishes just below the surface. As you stare, the train seems to sway to the rhythm of the water, and you feel as though you will sway right down into the depths. When you are in the middle of the lake, and it seems as if you are suspended alone above a solitary, watery planet, the train will travel very slowly. You will be grateful for this. If you are coming from New Orleans, you will release a long breath of relief as you pull into the old train station at Slidell.

The railroad played a vital role in the growth of Slidell. It was present before the Twin Spans or the Causeway ever connected the two shores of Lake Pontchartrain. Slidell's early development is also attributed to its brick industry. The city of Slidell is a product of all that is rich and natural found on the earth— the bounty of water, land, forests. Built on the edge of Lake Pontchartrain, the area teems with fishing, shrimping, and shipbuilding activity. Like countless groves of enormous Christmas trees, pine forests stand as sentinels throughout the Slidell area. The harmony of nature and the people who have settled in Slidell is depicted upon her flag.

The background of the flag, which was designed by Steven Higgs, is sectioned into three main areas by three green lines.

These represent the three interstate highways intersecting in Slidell, which brought people to the area to live. The top section on the flag is colored light blue in tribute to the wide skies that stretch over the city. On the lower part of the flag, a darker shade of blue is found and symbolizes the water that played such a significant role, past and present, in the town's development. In the center of the flag, the seal of the city is placed, filled with symbolism.

At the center of the circular seal, the history of the brick industry is represented by a corner of bricks inscribed with the Roman numeral for 1888, the year the town was founded. The fact that it is only a corner of bricks suggests that more building is to come in the future. The bricks sit at the shore of the lake, surrounded by pine trees. A single sailboat is upon the water and denotes the maritime and recreational boating of the area. Above the lake, the graceful arc of a rainbow rises, and was chosen to represent the cheerfulness of the people who inhabit Slidell.

Running in the foreground of the shield are the railroad tracks that preceded the interstates and helped give Slidell its life. Beneath the railroad track, one splendid rose-pink camellia blooms, proclaiming just how much the people of Slidell love her natural beauty. Slidell is known as the "Camellia City."

The circle is held together by cords of rope that signify the strong bonds of community and the earlier sailing and lumbering industries. A rim of gold that surrounds the circle is symbolic of the eternal ring of life. The words *Effort* and *Excellence* are found on banners, with arrows leading upwards from *Effort* to *Excellence*. This serves the dual purpose of showing that "effort leads to excellence," which is the motto of the people, and of paying tribute to the Indians who once dwelled on the shores of Lake Pontchartrain beneath the tall pine trees.

They, too, knew the importance of the delicate balance between nature and man.

An Essay on the
Designing of Flags

On March 4, 1861, the Committee on Flag and Seal made a report to the Provisional Congress of the Confederate States of America on its activities in selecting a design for the flag of the new nation. In its report, the committee observed:

> A flag should be simple, readily made, and, above all, capable of being made up in bunting. It should be different from the flag of any other country, place, or people. It should be readily distinguishable at a distance. The colors should be well contrasted and durable, and, lastly, and not the least important, it should be effective and handsome.

Simple, distinctive, handsome: these are the adjectives that should govern anyone who sets out to design a flag. Intricate designs should be avoided. Words should almost never be placed on a flag. Colors touching one another should contrast well.

Most countries adhere to these standards in their flags. More than 62 percent of the member countries of the United Nations have flags with simple features employing three colors or less. Only about 10 percent have features that are so complicated that a citizen would have difficulty making out his or her own country's flag.

Despite this simplicity of design, very few countries have identical flags. Little Monaco on the European side of the Mediterranean Sea shares a flag of red over white with Indonesia on the other side of the world. Since the Christmas Revolution in 1989 tore the badge of communism from its flag, Romania has joined Chad and Andorra in flying a blue, yellow, and red tricolor. These instances, however, are the exceptions that prove the rule.

Besides black and white, the most commonly used colors are

red, blue, green, and yellow. Bophuthatswana, India, Ireland, Ivory Coast, Niger, South Africa, and Zambia use orange in their flags, while Transkei is alone in the use of brown in its tricolor.

When one leaves the realm of national or federal flags, the observance of the rule of simplicity and distinctiveness is not as apparent. The flags of the American states are good examples, in many cases, of how not to design a flag. Some states, such as Alaska and Texas, have simple, distinctive, and handsome flags. Thirty-seven of the states, however, have more or less complex designs that employ the use of words or mottoes. Twenty states have merely placed the state seal or coat of arms on a blue field, and ten states have done so on a field other than blue.

Vexillography—the art of designing flags—is an offshoot of the ancient art of heraldry. In heraldic terms, "colors" include red, blue, and green, while white and yellow were termed "metals" to represent silver and gold. One of the earliest rules one learns in the study of heraldry is that color should not be placed on color, nor metal on metal. The practical reason for this is to provide for clarity and distinctiveness in a design.

Imagine a flag having a blue cross on a red field. While blue and red are certainly distinguishable colors, each is more sharply defined and distinctive if the blue cross is separated from the red field by a narrow white or yellow border. Likewise, if one pictures a flag composed of a yellow cross on a white field, it is clear that even at a short distance the cross will be hard to see, but if edged in a color, both the white and the yellow will be complemented.

When designing a flag, the theme should be kept simple. Many nations and movements use simple tricolor designs, either vertical, like the flag of France, or horizontal, as with the Lithuanian flag. In an effort to create more distinctive banners, geometric designs may be added to the tricolor field, such as the triangle found on the flags of the Bahamas and Sudan, or a perpendicular bar such as used on the flags of the Transvaal and the United Arab Emirates.

Many people wish to incorporate some distinctive emblem representative of their country or movement into their flag.

These too should be kept as simple as possible. Good examples of simplicity are the Canadian maple leaf and Israel's star of David.

Certain terminology is used to describe various parts and design elements of flags. The glossary in this book will help with some of this vocabulary.

Simple, distinctive, handsome: these words should be the hallmark of a flag. A flag is a statement, an artistic expression of a people or an idea. Like a good advertising trademark or political slogan, a well-designed flag should be identifiable at a glance.

Would you like to design a flag for your city, your parish, or your school?

From Flags of Tennessee *by Devereaux D. Cannon, Jr. (Gretna, La.: Pelican Publishing Company, 1990). Reprinted by permission of the author.*

91

The Art of Flag Making

It has long been felt, by most governments of the world, that in order to pay proper respect to a nation's flag, it must be made by hand. Nearly all flags are made of cloth. Which type of cloth is chosen depends on either the function or location of the flag.

Flags flown outdoors are usually made of a blend of nylon and wool, or other durable fabrics that are light and colorfast. For ceremonial occasions, the splendor of silk fabric is used to make the flag. For a long time, flag-makers used bunting, a strong woolen cloth. It was manufactured by mills in long strips that were nine inches wide. These strips were called breadths. Flags were measured by these terms. Cotton was used for less expensive flags, and has also been called bunting.

Making a flag can involve sewing, painting, embroidery, or appliqué. Pieces of material, or strips, are sewn together in the positions and sizes that compose the flag. The American flag is sewn together strip by strip. The white stars are first cut from cloth, then attached to the blue canton with one drop of glue to hold them in position. The stars are then further attached by sewing. The royal standard of Great Britain, and flags that are as complicated, are very often painted and embroidered completely by hand. The Canadian flag also combines sewing, hand-painting or appliqué, and sometimes embroidery.

Flags can be printed on paper or plastic, but this is usually done on paper. A silk-screen stencil is used separately for each color of the flag. Printed flags are not considered official by most governments.

When a flag is completed, a special machine punches holes at the bottom and top of the hoist. Metal rings are then placed into the holes, making the hoist strong enough to hold a flag on the halyard.

Glossary

ARMS: Composed of shield, crest, motto, and supporters. The shield is decorated with figures and colors that represent a family's distinction and accomplishments. Crests are feathers or tufts on birds' heads and are used to decorate the tops of the shields. Sometimes crowns are used to form the crest. Mottoes are the words that explain a family's motive in life, and are placed either on a scroll or on the actual shield. Supporters are living creatures, either human beings or animals, placed at both sides of the shield to support it. This tradition may stem from jousting tournaments. Knights entering a joust left their shields to be carried by two servants dressed as animals. Quartering the shield, as in the case of the Spanish flag Columbus carried, was done to combine the arms of two families. The first and fourth quarters were alike with one set of arms; the second and third quarters were also alike with the other family arms.

BADGE: Emblem.

BEARING: Any animal or other figure on a shield.

BORDER: An edging to a flag in a color different from the field of the flag, used either to prevent fraying or for decoration.

CANTON: Also known as the union of a flag, it is the upper left-hand corner of a flag. It is usually rectangular in shape. *Canton* is a French word meaning corner or angle.

CHARGE: To put a bearing—i.e., an animal or other figure— on a flag or a shield.

DEMILION: The upper half of a lion in an upright position. This is used as a charge.

DEXTER AND SINISTER: The right side of the shield is described as dexter; the left side is described as sinister. To an observer facing the shield, dexter would seem to appear to his left, while sinister would appear on his right.

DISPLAYED: A term used to describe any bird of prey appearing on a flag or shield with its wings spread and an exposed breast.

ENSIGN: The national flag used on a ship (a naval flag).

ESCUTCHEON: A shield or the complete coat of arms of a family. An *escutcheon of pretense* is a shield within a shield that displays an heiress's coat of arms.

FIELD: The color or background of a flag or shield. It is believed that the word originated from the days when the shields of knights were decorated with symbols that they had won on the field of battle.

FIMBRIATION: A thin edging, often white in color. Since the rules of heraldry forbid the placing of color on another color, a white fimbriation is used to separate different-colored components on a flag.

FLY: The length of a flag.

FLY END OR FLY EDGE: Terms used to denote the width of the flag at the point farthest from the staff.

GROUND: Another word for field.

HALYARDS: Ropes used to hoist and lower a flag and keep it in place.

HOIST: The width of the flag at the point closest to the staff.

JACK: A small flag showing nationality flown at the bow of a ship.

MULLET: A device from heraldry that now more commonly is referred to as a star, it usually has five points. Sometimes more points have been used.

ORIFLAMME: A banner or symbol depicting glory.

PASSANT: Used to describe lion walking with right paw raised.

RAMPANT: Used to describe an upright lion standing on one foot. If his head faces the observer, he is described as gardant. He is regardant if he is looking backward over the shoulder.

RESPECTANT: Two lions depicted upright and facing each other almost as if in combat.

ST. GEORGE'S CROSS: A cross in an upright "+" shape. It has been taken from the flag of England.

SALTIRE: Taken from the flag of Scotland, it is also referred to as a St. Andrew's cross. A saltire extends from corner to corner on a flag in an *X* shape.

STATANT: Used to describe a lion standing with all four paws on the ground.

TRUCK: The ornament on top of the flagstaff usually in the shape of a crown, cap, or knob. It is usually a circular piece of wood containing pulleys that control the halyards.

VEXILLOGRAPHY: The art of designing flags.

VEXILLOLOGY: Derived from the Latin word *vexillum*, which means flag, with the suffix *ology*, meaning "the study of." Simply defined, vexillology means "the study of flags."